A BUNCH OF SONNETS

By Dr. M. C. Gupta

(This page is intentionally left blank)

Table of Contents

Contents

PREFACE

I am an 82-year-old doctor who now practices as a lawyer. I was a professor of Medicine at the All India Institute of Medical Sciences (AIIMS), New Delhi. I later changed my profession and became a lawyer. I have authored books on Medicine as well as on Law, in addition to research papers in medical journals.

Poetry has been a serious hobby of mine. I have been writing poetry for a long time, both in English and Hindi. Fifteen of my Hindi poem books have already been published, mainly as Ghazals.

My first poetry book in English, titled War Poems, is currently in process of publication.

I write sonnets in the Shakespearean style. As per this style, a sonnet is classically a rhyming poem of fourteen lines written in iambic pentameter. The rhyming scheme is ABAB CDCD EFEF GG. The syllabic scheme is ten syllables in each line. The rhythm is iambic. Here the stress is on every second syllable (five beats of "da-DUM"). However, many sonnets, including mine, are unable to follow the iambic rhythm properly. In my case, the problem is not that I do not want to follow a rule rigidly. Rather, the problem is that English being my second language, I am not often able to discern and maintain the "da-DUM" beat.

Many of my sonnets have a spiritual angle and refer to God / Jesus. In this regard, I had to address the question- "Should we capitalise the pronouns referring to God or Jesus?"

Many of my sonnets have a spiritual angle and refer to God / Jesus. In this regard, I had to address the question- "Should we capitalise the pronouns referring to God or Jesus?"

Most of these sonnets have been published now and then on writing.com, an online community of authors. These have been written at different times. I have presented them here in a collated form. They have been arranged in the same sequence in which they were written. In my writing I've often preferred British spellings to the American ones.

Dr. M. C. Gupta

E-mail	mcgupta44@gmail.com
LinkedIn	https://www.linkedin.com/in/mcgupta44
WhatsApp / Mobile	+91-99993-33801

Typeset, Checked and Finalized by:

Nalin Savara

LinkedIn	http://www.linkedin.com/in/nsnsns
WhatsApp / Mobile	+91-9811109407 +91-95605-36188
E-mail	nsnsns@gmail.com (Often goes unchecked – use other modes to connect if can't reach via email)

1. THE FINAL MOMENT
[When the angel of death wins]

When all is done and Death, thy angel wins,
And brings me in His heavenly presence,
Then shall I beg that He forgive my sins,
And pray that I may be excused penance?

Then shall I let him know that I did try,
To follow His each and every command?
Or shall I to Him my acts justify,
So that I do not earn His reprimand?

I tried to do whatever He ordained.
I tried to follow that path which He showed.
What matters if my progress was restrained?
What, if I could not achieve as avowed?

I shall simply lay down myself prostrate,
At His feet and then for His judgment wait.

31st Dec. 2004

2. GOD'S WAYS

[About tsunami. God's ways are not known to man. We may fail in our logic, but never in our faith]

Should we lose faith in God because He kills,
Through ways that are so cruel to mankind?
Should we despise the gory wicked thrills,
He gets from His acts of tsunami kind?

Why can't He be kinder to His own sons,
Who worship Him and view Him with such awe?
Why can't He kiss and save the little ones?
Why should He them in fiery waters draw?

The logic of man cannot fathom out
His ways that are shrouded in mystery.
He simply keeps on wondering about
Why black events occurred in history.

Have faith in him and his perplexing ways.
He does look after his children always.

NOTE: A devastating tsunami occurred in India on 26 December 2004,

3rd Jan 2005

3. SUICIDE

[Who determines the final moment- He or man?]

Shall I leave my departure to my fate?
Or, shall I take decision on my own,
To end my life and leave the earthly gate,
When I feel that tired of life, I've grown?

Poor me! Why should such thoughts bother me so?
When my time comes, I won't have a moment,
To think whether to stay in world or go.
Why not let God his own wish implement?

When man has no power to avert death,
He can't have power to induce it, too.
Predestined is death by the Architect,
Who sent all of us to earth, me and you.

So, better give up all thought of suicide.
We must always by Him only abide.

4th Jan 2005

4. NEW YEAR WISH

[Why I don't send New Year greetings]

My friend, I do not feel like wishing you,
You, who are so sensible and seasoned.
Seasoned men don't care for a wish untrue,
Untrue is what so dislike the reasoned.

Reasoned men do never express a wish,
Wish that just cannot ever come about:
About catching in tsunami a fish.
Fish in troubled waters is rare no doubt!

Writ large is doubt in our own mind when we,
We wise ones of the educated kind,
Kind of offer wishes as in a spree,
Spree born of a rather unthinking mind.

Mind you that it is but for reason this,
This friend does not send happy New Year wish.

NOTE:
Written in a manner that each line starts with the end
word of the last line.

4th Jan 2005

5. MESSENGER

[Message from a hesitant lover]

My love, this note is meant to let you know,
That you are the queen of my dreary life.
I often dream I am taking a vow,
As I and you become husband and wife.

I know it's not a way to propose but,
Let this an honest explanation be:
I can't muster the courage in my gut,
To ask you for a date somewhere with me.

I hesitate, trepidation kills me,
The moment I consider this prospect.
My days, my weeks and months have gone empty,
In hope that my feelings you may suspect.

Let this uncertainty no more linger.
Let this sonnet be my true messenger.

6th Jan 2005

6. THANK YOU
[Thanks for breaking the heart]

Why should I not say thanks to you my friend,
That you have so fully broken my heart?
On hope no longer now it will depend,
When hope is doomed it will not come apart.

A broken heart is broken forever.
With each day more and more pain is added.
This friendship will return to me never,
Its thoughts in my mind will be embedded.

May you be happy in your venture new,
I hope I don't leave on your heart a scar.
Goodbye my friend, I wish good luck to you,
As I set out on my journey afar.

For giving me a lasting memory,
I thank you friend though I feel so sorry!

6th Jan 2005

7. WHAT IS POETRY?

[Poetry is that soothes the heart]

When thoughts are too deep for telling in prose,
When sentences and phrases can't suffice,
When words and feelings just cannot come close
Then recourse to poetry take the wise.

When words are overshadowed by meaning,
When logic overrides the expression,
When writer simply writes as he's dreaming
But rules of language mar his intention,

It's then that poetry assumes a shape,
When tears drip from a heart that's broken.
A poem consists not only of words,
Its each word is, of feelings, a token.

The wounds of heart a true poem does nurse.
What can't be healed by balm is healed by verse.

13th February, 2005

8. TOO MUCH TO ASK

[Is it too much to ask to be forgiven?]

Is it too much to ask you, O my Lord,
That you may forgive me each of my sin?
So far I have sown not peace but discord,
And have cheated even my kith and kin.

I have been unfaithful to my dear spouse,
I have not done to children my duty.
I should have been adorning my own house,
But, outside, I have been seeking beauty.

My heart has not thanked you for all you gave,
I have not bowed even once at your feet.
My Lord before I march unto my grave,
Before Death itself in hell does me greet,

I pray that you forgive this wayward soul.
Your forgiveness alone can make me whole.

22nd March 2005

9. BECKONING
[Beckoned by both Love and Death!]

Forever you're engraved within my heart,
No one can separate us, me and you.
Death can no longer play villainous part.
For you I too will embrace death, it's true.

Until I live, you will be mine always,
And when I quit this world we will be one.
We cannot understand God's hidden ways.
It was ordained that what He willed be done.

True love transcends barriers of this world,
We truly have been in touch all along.
Your soul is now free like a soaring bird,
To physical borders, you don't belong.

My love, for me please wait in the heavens.
I won't be late, Death's angel now beckons.

23rd March 2005

10. WATER DROP

*[On the grave water scarcity in many parts of the Indian
state of Rajasthan.]*

Some people are so deprived of water,
Others wallow in private swimming pools.
In future this will cause the wars rather,
Than oil, so tell the economics rules.

Drinking water is scarce in Indian states.
But Rajasthan suffers the maximum.
The rural people rue their tragic fates.
Dry wells are causing much social mayhem.

Women and men, the old and the young ones,
They watch the sky guessing the rain god's plan.
What can be done to cool the parching tongues,
In desert ridden Western Rajasthan?

For rural people's suffering to stop,
The urbanites must save each water drop.

NOTE: The motivation for writing this sonnet was the
first hand experience of acute water shortage in the
desert state of Rajasthan, especially its western part,
where the author spent six weeks as a consultant in an
international water project aimed at addressing the
water scarcity problem.

28th March 2005

11. OF RICHES, COATS AND CAMELS
[A reminder of Christ's preachings]

I won't pander to Mammon any more,
Enough has been my servitude to him.
Remember that Jesus too did implore:
If one is rich it is no doubt a sin;

A camel may get through the needle's eye,
But not a rich man through heavenly gate,
Give thy coat to one who has none say I,
Or devil will one day shadow your fate.

Why cling hard to this material clout?
An illusion it is, a passing show.
One day you will be quitting it no doubt,
Exhausted will be your days ere you know.

If salvation from this world you do want,
Then His name, in every breath, you must chant.

7th April 2005

12. REPENTANCE
[We must repent for our sins]

When all is lost and there is not a hope,
When no path shows itself and we are trapped,
Of escaping one does not find a scope
Energy is drained out and soul is sapped,

When life is living death and has no charm,
When one is left alone to rue the fate,
Then He extends to his children his arm
And from troubles he does them extricate.

We often are ready to blame the God.
He forgets each and every sinful deed.
Without seeking repentance from the Lord,
Salvation is impossible indeed.

O man thou better learn how to repent
For having life in sinful manner spent.

7th April 2005

13. I CANNOT RETREAT
[Expression of true love]

My love, you are attracted by others,
For me a thought or glance you cannot spare.
Soon you will be forsaken by lovers,
Their love is not like mine, so pure and rare.

Now you are enamoured of their beauty.
Fade up it will when their skin is wrinkled.
For my heart love is a call of duty.
My whole being is deep with your love sprinkled.

Ask your heart if you can live without me.
None else can love you so much as I do?
I don't have a desire but only this,
That I may give myself fully to you.

For you my heart does every moment beat.
I cannot from your love ever retreat.

9th April 2005

14. ONLY FOOLS LIKE ME

*[It is foolish to be distracted from the righteous path in
the face of ridicule]*

You say fools like me only tolerate,
Insults heaped on me by the tongues unkind.
I need not my innocence demonstrate,
To truth when my accusers are so blind?

Let me on my path fearless proceed,
Though it may be thorny and rather steep.
To sounds of caution why should I pay heed?
My commitment to Him I have to keep.

Though my mortal remains may lie in grave,
My soul has to yet reach up to Him higher.
Unsullied I must preserve what He gave.
Of my soul why Satan should be the buyer?

Without stopping you must go up the hill.
The day is done, the path untrodden still.

10th April 2005

15. GODLY MANIFESTATION

[Never give up faith. True faith is truly answered]

What can be done when hope itself is dead,
When all around is darkness, not a ray,
When soul of man by depression is led,
When old friends also shamelessly betray.

When kith and kin and one's own family,
Give up on one who is unfortunate,
When they even forsake him readily,
If so their own selfishness does dictate?

It's then divine benevolent support,
Suddenly shows up when not expected.
There comes a ship from nowhere in the port,
To rescue the doomed and the dejected.

Have faith in Him and put all doubt to rest.
God does in His wondrous ways manifest!

12th April 2005

16. HALF GLASS SYNDROME

*[Learn positive thinking. Count your blessings, not your
sorrows]*

When all is dark and troubles are galore,
When life is like a torture in prison,
When hope is gone, you can't take any more,
When travails come your way without reason.

When you led a proper and pious life,
But never for this you were rewarded,
When you did take care of the kids and wife,
But you were always blamed and discarded.

Then never should you blame the Creator.
You should not develop a temper ill?
Don't ever be the creation's hater.
There's plenty in life to be thankful still.

With half an empty glass why feel awful?
Thank Him your glass is as much as half-full.

26th April 2005

17. MOTHER ANGEL

[Mothers are real angels]

Are truly there any angels on earth?
Is this simply a myth that is untrue?
The word angel, does it have any worth?
Does its existence have a doubtful hue?

Ghosts and ghouls and spirits and the elves are,
Nothing but conjectures of the mankind.
That none has been sighted ever so far,
To this fact we cannot be ever blind.

But angels are from another realm,
Each one of us has experienced this.
Mother's touch makes a child in anguish calm,
Her touch is so full of a divine bliss.

Yes, mothers are truly angels of God.
They represent Him; angels are no fraud.

15th May 2005

18. TURN OF FATE

[Happiness is a state of mind, often independent of externalities]

Why lament that He gave you so much pain?
Why think pleasures you have few and meagre?
Why wish to have joys again and again?
Why for a painless life be so eager?

Don't think that you are burdened the utmost,
Just look around, you'll find it is not true.
Some people are rich and of treasures boast,
But they too have troubles they always rue.

Life's pleasure needs to be balanced with pain.
Pleasure and pain are sides of the same coin.
In mind only are thoughts of loss or gain.
Why should we ever ranks of mourners join?

Wisdom tells us it is the state of mind,
That marks a turn as pleasant or unkind.

24th May 2005

19. SACRIFICE FOR HIM

[Life is short and we live but once. Shun pleasures and make sacrifice for His sake]

He sent us to this world so that we may,
Devote ourselves to fulfil His command,
While doing so do not quiver or sway,
Though Satan may make unholy demand.

It's not easy to resist temptation,
Or always in actions be righteous.
Though all of us desire our salvation,
To sacrifice, we are oblivious.

For pleasure of finally meeting Him,
The worldly pleasures we must sacrifice.
We must learn not to live as per our whim,
We shall not come to live in this world twice.

O man, think of Him every day and hour,
So that by grace He may your sins cover.

30th June 2005

20. NEXT MOMENT

*[Man cannot be sure of the next moment, the next
breath. It is better to live in the present than plan for the
future]*

One moment we are so bubbling with life,
The next moment we mingle in the dust.
Though much we are attached to home and wife,
Quitting all of these one day is a must.

Though we may for tomorrow have a hope,
It's never guaranteed to anyone.
With present only can we ever cope,
Of future certain there can be no one.

Why plan for many a decade ahead?
Of your next breath even you can't be sure.
Be contented with whatever you've had.
Amass not riches every day yet more.

Riches will take you away yet farther,
From gates of heaven and from your Father.

4th September 2005

21. MONEY WORSHIP

[A man is respected only as long as his pocket is full]

Why did I have to come across the day,
When I'm alone, I have no company?
My friends have all suddenly turned away,
Forsaking me in my final journey?

At one time I too was much sought after,
When people vied to come along with me.
Their smile to me could not have been brighter,
For them I was the ideal to be.

Why all my friends did discard me and throw?
They were not after me but my money.
But now that I have all of it let go,
They find a pauper's company funny.

Money is a big evil Jesus said.
Yet worshipped by man it is, it's so sad.

24ᵗʰ September 2005

22. LIFE IS NOT A BED OF ROSES

*[Journey together can be pleasant only when the two
have faith and they support, not suspect, each other]*

My love, life is not a bed of roses.
One cannot always have only pleasures.
In fact the reality imposes:
We get losses, too, not only treasures.

We both are really new in this game.
The ways of life are by us untrodden.
We should not each other needlessly blame,
If our days are presently so rotten.

Come, let us support each other and not,
Submit ourselves to gnawing depression.
Though now adversity may be our lot,
Let us not have a sense of rejection.

Let us have faith and hope in Him always,
Though we can't often understand his ways.

24th September 2005

23. DESTINATION

[This world is a mirage. His is the real world and He the
destination]

This world is but really a mirage,
A passing show that is temporary.
Superficial is every visage,
Though some people do have views contrary.

Those who think that the real world is this,
They dwell in it mentally all the time.
But those who think the real world is His,
Consider His worship their duty prime.

Those who worship Him follow His command,
To be helpful to all and love others.
If they don't, they know He would reprimand,
For them it is His kingdom that matters.

Live life but entangled in it don't be.
Don't forget your destination is He.

24th September 2005

24. ONE SIDED LOVE
[What happens when the lover is too shy]

In one moment crazy so long ago,
I fell in love with a beautiful girl.
Whenever a glance at me did she throw,
In heady love my heart did truly swirl.

My eyes followed her till the very end,
My feet traced every inch that she did walk.
Yet outwardly I did always pretend,
As if at the name of love I did balk.

But my dream was one day truly shattered;
I saw her by the side of another.
In vain myself I had always flattered,
That my own love would also afflict her.

Too late I did this simple lesson learn:
If we don't throw a ball it can't return.

5th October 2005

25. MEETING IN HEAVEN

[A hope that one may meet the departed one in heaven]

Though now you are gone never to return,
You continue to live yet in my thoughts.
The flame of life only for you does burn.
On my heart's door your memory still knocks.

I do live but only half a life now.
In body and mind I am incomplete.
Without you I just don't exist somehow.
With loneliness my world is now replete.

A day will come when I will be no more,
I hope that day is not delayed too long.
I'm already in the yonder world your,
To this world I no longer do belong.

One day, my love, again we shall be one.
If He wishes, we shall meet in heaven.

20th October 2005

26. WHEN MY TURN COMES

[All of us shall have our turn. Why fear it?]

When my turn comes to bid goodbye to all,
And start afresh on a journey unknown,
Shall such change I endeavour to forestall,
Because it may be painful and forlorn?

Shall I look forward to what lies ahead?
Or, shall I lament and pine for my past?
Of future, shall I be too much afraid?
Or, shall I joyfully uphold the mast?

Often we cry when we ought to rejoice.
Often we treat a shadow as a ghost.
We fail to listen to our inner voice.
That which has gone we often miss the most.

Surprisingly in this drama of life,
Against ourselves we sometimes wield the knife.

21st October 2005

27. WHEN I SAY FINAL GOODBYE

*[The last moment is best spent thinking of Him rather
than the world around us]*

When my turn comes to say final goodbye,
And cast a parting look on those around,
Shall I utter a weak and helpless sigh?
Shall there be tears in my hopeless eyes found?

Shall I tell them for one last time again,
To take care of what all I leave behind?
Shall I crave for a pill to ease my pain?
Shall I be totally blank in my mind?

I wish that if He grants me consciousness,
During my last moments, I may thus pray:
"To serve you I have not been effortless.
To you I have nothing but this to say-

Forgive me for the sins I committed,
Though I have others for their sins hated".

21st October 2005

28. THE IMAGE OF WOMAN

[There are many aspects of womanhood. Which is the most distinctive?]

What makes a woman distinct from a man?
Is it her beauty, tender, yet divine,
By which she entraps only as she can,
Making him for her love forever pine?

Is it her touch that is so sweet and soft,
Which makes the hearts of the hardest men melt?
It's said of women very truly oft,
That cruelty in them cannot be felt.

Though all this is true of women yet I,
Say that the real difference is this:
In her bosom a mother's heart does lie,
In this she does fulfil a Godly wish.

If women downplay motherly image,
Who else can then their own image salvage?

21st October 2005

29. LIVE IN THE PRESENT

[It is no use trying to reconstruct the past or plan the future.]

Why try to reconstruct a broken dream?
Why try to convert past into future?
Why try to churn water, expecting cream?
Why try to rein the forces of nature?

A broken heart can never be made whole.
What happened once can never be undone.
Something impossible can't be a goal.
By man the nature can't be ever won.

It's wiser not to try to play the god.
It's better that we do the task in hand.
It's saner not to past and future prod.
It's safer that we walk on solid land.

Man should do his duty in the present.
Else later he would his actions resent.

25th October 2005

30. WILMA, RITA, KATRINA
[Can they subdue man?]

Man cannot by a Wilma be humbled,
Nor he can by Rita be thrown off guard.
He cannot by Katrina be crumbled,
He's not afraid of the El Nino's sword.

He made man truly in his own image,
To rule the world that lies under his feet.
Man can't by nature be held in bondage.
From rock and sea he can't accept defeat.

Upheavals in earth and ocean cannot,
Displace man from his own abode on land.
With courage he will be able to win,
As long as he has his logic at hand.

God does support man's confidence in self.
But, foolish man, don't confront God Himself.

NOTE: WILMA, RITA and KATRINA were category 5
cyclones that occurred in 2005 and caused much
devastation.

26ᵗʰ October 2005

31. HALLOWEEN
[The departed spirits visit us on this day]

Our dearest ones are all departed now.
Their memory lingers yet in the heart.
They gave us all their best but we somehow,
Have yet to return their love on our part.

How much we wish they were with us again,
So that once more the olden days are back.
We remember times of pleasure and pain.
Their company throughout the life we lack.

As if truly in answer to our wish,
Those who have left us come back on this day.
Halloween is the day when in impish
Manner the spirits come to us and say:

Don't think we are impotent and dead yet.
We do tricks so you may not us forget.

26th October 2005

32. THE CRICKET OF LIFE
[Life is like a game of cricket]

The life is simply like a cricket game,
Where players come and play their own inning.
They try to gather runs and make a name,
Batting or fielding, constantly running.

They hit the ball and manage a few runs,
They think that they have built up a treasure.
They beat aloud their own victory drums,
Forgetting it is a fleeting pleasure.

In his hurry man forgets that the next
Ball may be destined to be but the last.
As he raises the bat to show his best,
The ball reaches the stumps and makes a blast.

A few only do make a century.
Just, play your inning well and don't hurry.

8th January 2006

33. THE FINAL DAY
[Shall it be a day of mourning or rejoicing?]

A day will come when I shall be no more,
I shall not breathe the fragrance of this earth.
That day may be delayed but will come sure.
Then I shall be beyond all woe or mirth.

All whom I love and who love me today,
Will one day be beyond my reach or grasp.
They'll put me in my grave and go away.
I shall have none but my own hand to clasp.

Shall that be a day of mourning for me,
When I cast my worn-out mortal raiment?
No, if one day from this world I am free,
I would enter His kingdom that moment.

Shall I lament quitting this lowly world?
Or, rejoice that I go to hear His word?

10th January 2006

34. TEMPERANCE

[It is better to be temperate than harsh]

Shall I stoop, too, because you have done so,
Hitting below the belt and mouthing foul?
No, I would, in fact, let you rather know,
I shall not roar in response to your growl.

It's easy to hit back in anger wild,
Eye for an eye is, but, too barbaric.
Why not answer the harsh by gestures mild?
Why not meet cacophony with lyric?

A bark cannot a caravan withhold.
A thorn cannot cause a rose to wither.
The meek shall inherit the earth, not bold.
A smile, rather than a frown is better.

God, impart me a bit of your fragrance.
May I follow the path of temperance.

17th January 2006

35. WINTERS OF LIFE
[Winters in various stages of life]

When winter comes and snow is all around,
It casts a spell in ways quite different.
Children enjoy playing in icy ground,
For them winter is an event transient.

The young find warmth in each other's embrace,
As they savour choicest whisky and wine.
For them winter has a beautiful face,
They truly make merry and dance and dine.

The old are the ones for whom winter brings,
A cold and bitter message that is sure.
A stark truth in their mind bitterly rings:
"In old age winter is hard to endure.

You witnessed many a spring and summer.
But winter, you are just meant to suffer".

21st January 2006

36. WHEN I SHALL PASS BY
[I too will go one day.]

A day will come when I too shall pass by.
No longer will my shadow haunt the world.
To meet my dear ones however I try,
Will be something impossible, unheard.

I know not where I shall henceforth be gone,
Nor what in nether world would be my fate.
Shall I forever in hell fire be thrown?
Or, shall I albeit enter heaven's gate?

Whatever be the fate I need not dwell,
In future while living in the present.
For miles I have to go before I tell:
My time is up, the Lord has for me sent.

Lord I have tried my best to do your bid.
With faith in you, I have done all I did.

22nd January 2006

37. WHAT WE DON'T SEE
[What we see may not be the true picture.]

All that we see need not always be true.
Of this we must ourselves always remind.
The sky and sea are, from distance, so blue.
But, go nigh them and no colour you find.

The outward is often a sham, a mask,
Worn so that what's inside may be concealed.
Before the outer fools us, we must ask:
'Does this cloak have daggers yet unrevealed?'

What we don't see may still, in fact, exist,
But may be seen only by those gifted.
Enroll in His true, selfless workers' list,
The veil from your eyes will then be lifted.

By His grace the lame can, mountains, conquer.
The dumb, too, can eloquent speech render.

NOTE:
The last two lines have been translated from:

"mook hoee vaachaal,
Pangu chadhaee girivar gahan"

[Famous lines in Ram Charit Maanas, a revered religious
text of Hindus, written in Hindi language.]

18th February 2006

38. MAKE IT HAPPEN
[My spirit is weak. Lift it]

So said Jesus: Don't covet what's your friend's,
Nor cast a vile eye on your neighbour's wife.
He bid man to shun all stealthy errands,
And not to depose false when there is strife.

O Lord, your commandments, I know by heart,
Yet each of them I have broken so far.
In your service I never played my part,
In worship of Satan I knew no bar.

I wasted life's long years that you gave.
My flesh and spirit are both of them weak.
How can I, from hell, ever myself save?
I can, humbly, my Lord, only thus speak:

"O Lord, you alone can make this happen,
You can still send this sinner to heaven".

26th February 2006

39. PICK UP THE DICE
[Time never comes back. Act NOW]

Why keep gazing forever at the dice?
Why wait for the most opportune moment?
Prevarication is a mental vice,
It adds only to one's predicament.

Can he who keeps sitting at river bank,
Learn swimming without entering water?
One must jump in and be quite bold and frank.
He only wins who just does not falter.

The wise ought to be quite careful that,
We waste not what we can't ever regain.
Let thriftiness be our guiding diktat,
Let saving each minute be our refrain.

Let's pick up the dice, roll it and just throw.
Do not keep sitting in the waiting row.

27th February 2006

40. MARCH OF TIME
[Time never stops; nor should we]

When all is gone and I am reduced to
Nothing more than an ounce of rotting dust,
You too will forget me one day it's true.
Why should remembering me be a must?

We love but our love can't be permanent;
The march of King of Time is unfettered.
It nibbles one by one every moment
Of present, which, in the past, is treasured.

My love, when one day you find me no more,
I hope you move ahead from where we are.
A fit tribute it would be for me sure.
I shall wish you all success from afar.

The march of time is unending, constant.
We must keep on moving every moment.

3rd March 2006

41. THE PROUD MAN
[Is man superior to animals?]

Is man superior to animals?
Are animals inferior to him?
On going through evolution's annals,
Such thoughts are nothing but the proud man's whim.

Real superiority lies in
The power to defeat adversity.
On this count cockroach would easily win.
It has survived too much calamity.

The man on the other hand so quickly
Is destroying himself and mother earth,
And causing much pollution so freely
That one does doubt his ecologic worth.

Man, be not proud that He will favour you.
The creator has other creatures too.

NOTE:
Cockroaches are an enormously ancient and successful
group of insects. Cockroaches were one of the very first
terrestrial insects, appearing during the early
Carboniferous era some 280 million years ago.

3rd March 2006

42. DOOR OF DEATH

[We all have to pass through this door. Why worry?]

As time passes the young become the old
And one day, from the drama, we are gone.
Before all mysteries of life unfold,
The door of death we are cruelly shown.

To hell or heaven which way we shall go,
To none of us this can ever be known.
As icy winds in winter of life blow,
The door of death we are cruelly shown.

If we don't know our fate then why lament?
We came alone and we shall go alone.
None will save us in the final moment.
The door of death we are cruelly shown.

As time passes the young become the old.
The door of death we are cruelly shown.

NOTE: This is a Kyrielle Sonnet. It differs from the usual
sonnet in that the last line of the first stanza is used as a
refrain repeated at the end of each subsequent stanza
and the final couplet.

16th March 2006

43. WHEN TIME IS UP

[In order to be happy, learn to be contented]

When time is up and the curtain is down
And exit from the world is what is due;
Shall I walk down the path having a frown?
Or, shall the fate that befell me I rue?

Shall I lament that I could not enjoy,
What like a honey bee I gathered hard?
Of prolonging life shall I think some ploy?
Shall I try once again a tarot card?

No I shall thank the Lord he gave me all
That I needed in generous measure.
I shall not heed the greedy Satan's call,
Who wants me to incur His displeasure.

Happiness can never be invented.
It comes itself when we are contented.

2nd April 2006

44. LOVE
[Real love is deep. Sex is superficial]

The emotion that's love is but unique,
It just cannot be kindled or be killed.
It comes from heart and does not bear critique,
It has been as man's strongest power billed.

In love one can truly give one's own life,
In love one can take another life too.
For husband, sacrifices does make wife,
Husbands also love their wives, it is true.

But when love is another name for sex,
It loses its power that is divine.
When its value is paid in bills or cheques,
It turns from spirit to the cheapest wine.

The bonds of love are deep in the heart laid.
It's not love if it's sought to be repaid.

9th April 2006

45. FROZEN FLAME
[Sublimation of unrequited love]

How long shall I wait that my love may come
One day from somewhere unknown, unannounced?
My heart has over time too old become.
All feelings of love from it have been trounced.

The flame of love cannot be rekindled,
It, too, resides in but a mortal frame.
In course of time it too does get dwindled,
Remaining though a flame only in name.

A frozen flame cannot be ignited,
Nor can the frozen heart resound a beat.
By darkness dark can never be lighted,
To youth, old age must one day give its seat.

Shall I repent that love could not be mine?
No Lord, I have your love. I know you're mine.

9th April 2006

46. PARDON US
[Pardon and help us, O Lord]

When life is bleak with not a ray of hope,
When night is dark with not a single star;
When with the pain inside we cannot cope,
When heart is full of too many a scar;

When death is more colourful than the life,
When enemies look better than the friends;
When ungratefulness stabs us like a knife,
When love does not return despite amends;

Then do we feel so utterly helpless.
Then we truly remember You, O Lord.
Then do we bow at your feet and express
Our prayer to you of our own accord.

Your hallowed greatness lies, O Lord, in this:
Please pardon us and grant our humble wish.

21st April 2006

47. SHE WAS NOT LIFE BUT DEATH

[When beauty turns into beast]

In my life she came like a ray of hope,
A wisp of fresh breeze in a stagnant space,
As if, for drowning man, to catch a rope.
I was faceless, she had a pretty face!

She brought life to my dull and rotting life;
She filled it with a happiness unknown.
She brought serenity in place of strife;
With happy smiles she did replace my groan.

I know not truly what later transpired.
Why did I earn, full of poison, her ire?
Her face, no more pretty, no hope inspired.
The cool and sweet turned into hellish fire.

As I lay stabbed waiting for my last breath,
I realized, not life, but she was death.

23rd April 2006

48. DILEMMA
[The dilemma of how to profess one's love]

I don't know why I cannot forget you,
Though all else I do forget now-a-days.
If it is love then do you love me, too?
Or is it one of my empty forays?

If it's love that has taken hold of me,
How shall my feelings be to you conveyed?
I can't remain silent like a dummy;
To say to you "I love you", I'm afraid.

This dilemma is certainly killing.
How can one be silent and yet vocal?
I knew not that love can be so grilling.
My heart is caught in confusion total.

They say true love can never be hidden.
May you divine that I am so smitten.

27th April 2006

49. THE OLD AND THE YOUNG

[They think differently]

The old say that the young are not like them;
They don't have wisdom, hard work they don't do.
Such thoughts in their mind do really stem
From this belief they're always right and true.

They forget that the world is of the young,
And that they themselves are on the way out.
The fact is that their place is now among
Those who have no substance, but, only clout.

The old lament the young don't show respect.
They forget that respect is commanded.
If motives of the old seem too suspect,
The young may hold back respect demanded.

With advancing age old men ought to learn:
The young's respect is but for them to earn.

1ˢᵗ May 2006

50. IS FALLING IN LOVE A FOLLY?
[Falling in love, even in failed love, is worth it]

Is falling in love a folly indeed?
No, it's expression of a vibrant heart.
To love someone is not simply a creed.
In fact, it is the most difficult art.

Some love, but their love is not requited.
Are they the losers? Don't they gain something?
Better, in love, remain un-united,
Than remain outside Cupid's following.

Though we may be, in love, unsuccessful,
The fever of love is memorable.
It exerts on the mind a silken pull,
To ignore which we may not be able.

Do not sit by the pool of love, waiting.
Dive and swim, do not be hesitating.

1st May 2006

51. BE UP AND RUNNING
[The fruit of action comes to those who act]

Shall I sit on the shore afraid to swim?
Why simply watch with awe the gushing waves?
Shall my desire to surf remain a whim
Of someone who is afraid but yet craves?

For how long shall I harbour a vain hope
That magic would somehow show on its own?
But wishful thinking has in life no scope.
Why should I, towards reveries, be prone?

Those only get the prize who dare and dive,
Not those who dream of pearls, basking on shore.
Of honey, full in winter is the hive,
'Cause bees gathered in summer nectar pure.

Be up and running, don't waste a moment.
None knows when he will quit mortal raiment.

3rd May 2006

52. THE ORIENTAL MYSTIQUE
[The culture of the East is distinctive]

What, after all, is the Eastern mystique?
What mental images does the East bring?
Is it the black magic and the rope trick?
Is it the elephant or jungle king?

Is it the half -clad monk with shaven head?
Women in veil, too shy to show their face?
The child who starves simply for lack of bread?
Queens attired in pure silk and golden lace?

All this is East but in reality,
A way of life it is, cultural prism,
That's steeped deep in spirituality,
Away from outward materialism.

That East is East and West is West was said
By Kipling who had been in the West bred.

NOTE: Rudyard Kipling wrote in his The Ballad of the
East and West:
"Oh, East is East, and West is West, and never the twain
shall meet"

6th May 2006

53. DREAMS OF FUTURE

[Live in the present, not the past or the future]

Why thoughts of future now I should harbour?
Why should I plan the shape of things to come?
It's no use worrying about the future
Why should the future be so bothersome?

Shall I design my moves as playing chess
On this chess board, the canvass of my life?
Shall I think, now, by what name I'll address
My future son and daughter and my wife?

No, this is all mere worthless day-dreaming.
This game of chess is pre-planned already
By Him who's always kind and well- meaning.
My every move for me He has ready.

We should all the time live in the present.
Why dream of future, or the past repent?

19th May 2006

54. SHOULD I REPENT?
[Should I repent that I did waste my life?]

Should I repent that I did waste my life,
Which I could have put to much better use?
Should I be sorry I fought with my wife,
And gave her less of love, more of abuse?

Should I lament my children don't adore
Their dad as much as they dote on their mom?
Should I in my heart feel bitter and sore
That in my old age I sleep in a dorm?

No, why should I, by all this, be rattled?
Shall I not bid goodbye to all one day?
In fact it is the nature's law settled,
That ultimately one would lie in clay.

Why aspire for pleasure till comes the end?
Why not welcome the pain that god does send?

20th May 2006

55. THE PRAYER WHEEL
[About the Buddhist Prayer Wheel]

Let this prayer wheel continue its whirl;
Let His praise be chanted every moment.
The flag of His glory you must unfurl;
It must keep up spiritual ferment.

O monk, with ochre robe and shaven head,
A prayer bead garland in the left hand,
Moving the wheel with right hand as you tread,
You enlighten all in a sacred land.

Busy truly you are, His messenger,
His peace and serenity on your face.
To all you verily do deliver,
His true wisdom and His bountiful grace.

O monk, O priest, O swami, I beseech:
To me also kindly his message preach.

20th May 2006

56. WEDDING ADVICE
[An important message for couples]

I do rejoice that you are now wedded
To one who has been always in your thought;
Whose image in your heart is embedded,
Who has a real change in your life brought.

While everyone celebrates your wedding,
And gives you flowers, bouquets and the gifts,
My friend, I tell you an important thing
To tackle much of marital conflicts:

"In marriage happiness does not depend
On finding a good partner in your life.
What matters is: spouses must learn to bend,
And be themselves a good husband or wife".

This is the key, my friend, to happiness.
Ignore it and life will be in wilderness.

4th June 2006

57. THANK YOU, LORD
[Singing the Lord's praise]

I thank you Lord that you have given me
A body, mind, a soul and tender heart.
Please enable me to clearly see
What duties I must fulfil on my part.

Your bounty is so much overwhelming,
I don't know how I can repay your debts.
Do not make me leave this world repenting
That I could not rise up from lowly depths.

Lord, kindly change my life into a mould
That makes me an instrument of your peace.
Awaken me so that I may behold
Your omnipresence in mountains and seas.

Grant me that I may in no case afford
To forget you for a moment, O Lord.

6th June 2006

58. CALL ME UNTO YOU

*[As my soul quits this bodily frame, I'll wait again for
Your orders, Lord]*

My eyes will be one day closed on this world,
A vaster one will open then to me,
Where one will not depend on written word;
Communication will be language- free.

I shall be free from bodily constraints
That pose impediment to free movement.
My soul will then move free without restraints,
Without man-made walls of concrete, cement.

I will have no desire or earthly wish.
I will be simply doing His errand.
Whether it be man, beast or fowl or fish,
I will be truly all His creatures' friend.

Lord, when you think my task on earth is done,
Call me to your feet for a job new one.

22nd August 2006

59. LIFE IS LIKE A SCHOOL
[We keep on learning at every stage of life]

Bard did say that man's life is like a stage,
But I say it is much more like a school.
Throughout life from birth till the ageing days,
We keep on adding to our knowledge pool.

We learn as a toddler to avoid fire.
We learn as a young man to court a flame.
As we grow old we learn to curb desire
And lead a life that is devoid of blame.

The real knowledge that we ought to learn
Often escapes us till we breathe our last:
To learn that we must serve Him and thus earn
That which will stay with us when life is past.

As from the school of life we graduate,
We must learn to love all, to no one hate.

15th September 2006

60. PARTING

[A couple parts company without rancour]

My dear we do part company today,
Each other's presence we just can't endure.
It's just that our life went a bit astray.
It does not mean we don't love any more.

Let's watch out we don't start a new blame game.
That will not serve any useful purpose,
Except that it will surely bring bad name;
A stigma would attach to both of us.

The path of love has always been smoothless.
Love started once cannot be guaranteed.
When acrimony is beyond redress,
Why not from this shallow bond we be freed?

Let's be thankful for those good days we spent.
Let's not for the bad days spent now repent.

27th September 2006

61. MONSTERS

[The monsters of memories take away the peace of mind]

Be silent, you monsters of memories.
I can't endure your jabbing any more.
Calm down and let my mind be at some ease.
You've tortured me enough through vileness your.

You reflect all that in the past I did,
Or what others have done in life to me.
The past is past and now I do forbid:
Don't play these games so evil and dirty.

Let me forget the past and look ahead.
Let me live now only in this instant.
I wish you, monsters of memory, dead.
For such cursing, never would I repent.

I can't have peace as long as you're alive.
I banish you. Go, die. Let me survive.

3rd October 2006

62. DON'T MAKE ME A WOMAN
[Feelings of many women in a male dominated world]

God don't make me a woman in next life,
No more I want to be tortured by men.
A woman's life is full of woe and strife.
She's subjected to all sort of mayhem.

She's killed unborn while she is in the womb.
If born, it is the girl who is fed less.
Till she gets her final rest in the tomb,
She faces much cruelty and distress.

It may be in the East or in the West,
Male ego always does deprive women.
Men always corner for themselves the best,
Forgetting they were once mothers' children.

Why say God made in his image the man?
That credit ought to go to the woman.

19th October 2006

63. DREAMS ONCE SHATTERED

[Dreams may be shattered. But don't stop dreaming]

Once dreams are shattered they can't be rebuilt;
By no means can we gain what has been lost.
Just as misdeeds can't be undone by guilt,
Of dead dreams one can never pay the cost.

Life's full of many a hurdle and pain,
To forget which we weave our silken dreams.
But if they're shattered we cannot regain,
The joy of glittering colourful gleams.

If dreams are shattered, take care that, in turn,
You don't become yourself heartless and cold.
The flame of love in a young heart does burn.
It must be kept up though you may grow old.

You must not cease to dream till your last day.
It's dreams that keep unhappiness away.

26th October 2006

64. SLIPPING AWAY

*[Feelings of the lover when he / she knows that the
partner is slipping away]*

Although I hold you tight against my breast,
I know your heart is no longer with me.
The days are gone when you could not arrest
Your racing heart when me you used to see.

I know you are slipping away from me.
I know that now I cannot hold you back.
I know now from me you want to be free.
I know our bond has now suffered a crack.

But what I don't know is the reason why
Now you have dumped both me and my friendship.
Why did you want to give my love a try
When well you knew that one day you would slip?

Despite all this I don't want to lose you.
May such feeling god put in your heart too.

27th October 2006

65. SEND ME TO HELL

[Better send me to hell than to earth as a woman next time—a woman's prayer]

God, I do worship at your feet and pray,
A girl not be born to me in next life.
I've got only this much, O God, to say,
Send me to hell instead, save me this strife.

A female's life is steeped too much in woe;
The very day she's conceived is a curse.
To male ego she often has to bow
And through her life this grievance does she nurse.

Though it's a trend prevalent everywhere,
The women in the East are more oppressed.
Laws banning female foeticide are there;
In practice, though, they are often transgressed.

I hope one day women freely do live
As equals and be thanked for what they give.

NOTE:
The first stanza is the translation of a folk song in Hindi in the North Indian state of Uttar Pradesh. This song depicts the harsh reality of female subjugation, reflected in a mother's prayer to god that he may not give her a daughter in her next life.

प्रभु जी मैं तोरी बिनती करूं, पैय्यां पड़ूं बार बार
अगले जनम मोहे बिटिया न दीजे, नरक दीजे चाहे डार

Prabhu jee main toree binatee karoon, paiyaan padoon baar baar
Agale janam mohe bitiyaa na deeje, narak deeje chaahe Daar
A reader wrote to me as follows:
"The writing is both heart and mind blowing. The eyes get filled with tears while reading it. The true emotions of a suffering woman's and her guardians' suffering mind have been shown like a picture."

29th October 2006

66. FAMILY OR LIVE IN?

[A live-in relationship is no substitute for a family]

It's difficult to say what virtue is
And what, in fact, does constitute a vice.
It's no use if we debate this topic;
In my view saying this much will suffice:

The young want the company of someone
For love and pleasure that he or she gives.
But yet commitment they want to have none.
It's through commitment, a society lives.

Without a family there is no home.
A home means sons, daughters and the parents.
Outside countries like US, England, Rome,
The live-in a society resents.

Why avoid one's responsibility?
Is family such a difficulty?

10th November 2006

67. ROBIN HOOD

[There must be some reason why Robin Hood is still remembered]

There must be some reason why Robin Hood,
The King of Outlaws is remembered still.
Though he had no respect for legalhood
For his men the law was his every will.

Though many legends does his name unfold,
The "Golden Arrow" one is most famous.
The Prince of Thieves, as he was often called,
Said to his seven score merry men thus:

"For the Nottingham Sheriff I care not.
My writ runs large in the Sherwood Forest.
The rich may think my name is just a blot.
For poor people, I do for them what's best".

That's why he was the hero of his day,
And continues as such even today.

21ˢᵗ November 2006

68. WEDDED TO POETRY

[I lost my wife and then got wedded to poetry]

It's easy to blame God for all our ills
But we forget what he has given us.
Our needs he as per his planning fulfils,
But we in our ignorance make a fuss.

He only knows what is His grand design
Which he has planned for the rest of our life.
Why wish that all the days we get sunshine,
Why should a rainy day cause mental strife.

When he takes something he gives another
He did so to me, this I can't forget.
I lost my wife causing me to shatter.
But, gift of poetry I did then get.

Although God has taken away my wife,
To poetry I am wedded for life.

21st November 2006

69. EXPECTATIONS

*[Others have their own problems. Try to help them
rather than seek their help]*

We often lament we are not well cared
By friends and acquaintances in our life.
But they too are not from their problems spared.
They also have in their own life much strife.

It's true that we need others' love and care,
But do we give the same to those others?
It's too uncommon, almost rather rare
To find one who for others' sake suffers.

Why not the others' wounds we learn to heal
Before expecting them to heal our own?
The pain of others we should try to feel
And not in front of all, just cry and moan.

No man can be an island to himself.
Ere seeking help, help others and yourself.

8th December 2006

70. DO GOOD AND BE BLESSED
[Man can wash off his sins by doing good deeds]

May God soften hearts that are made of stone
And make tender thoughts sprout where grimness rules.
May God bless them who to sinning are prone
And shape them into his own godly tools.

May God change the unimpressionable
Hearts into those that feel the others' pain.
Let his kindness verily enable
Humans to love others and shed disdain.

Sinner a man may be born but why he
Should go one day from this world yet in sin?
By doing good he can from sins be free.
All that he needs is to be clean within.

Do good and you shall truly earn his grace.
Else, you shall consequences of sin face.

11th January 2007

71. MY FIRST CRUSH
[The futility of and inability to forget my first crush]

No, I just cannot forget my first crush,
When I grew out of childhood into teens,
When with another heart I had a brush,
My heart had got broken to smithereens.

What lofty dreams I had at that young age!
Nothing else in those days I thought about.
What blessing was that temporary craze!
Its futility I did soon find out.

But this I must admit that my first crush,
Despite the fact that my hair is now gray,
Does still make me in a mild manner blush,
When I'm lost in old memories someday.

About it I do not have a regret.
It's true that my first love I can't forget.

2nd February 2007

72. AN ODE TO THE COW
[In praise of the cow, a motherly symbol in Hinduism]

You silent creature sent by god on earth
To feed your milk to man in his childhood,
And thereby give him nature's joy and mirth,
Denied to him by drying motherhood!

O cow, you feed the child of him who kills
Because he finds that your flesh is tasty.
With your milk though his child's tummy he fills,
He subjects you to cruelty nasty!

O dear cow, you are so non-violent,
To harm you is a sin against the god.
To kill one who is so benevolent,
Is truly on mother nature a fraud.

Why can't man let other animals live?
Why can't he, to animals, his love give?

4th March 2007

73. BLUE SKY AND DARK SHADOWS
[Memories of the past, retained by one of the lovers]

Remember when the sky was vast and blue,
Resplendent with many a floating cloud?
Life every day had a different hue;
"Enjoy", life had a message clear and loud.

Remember when a million lamps did dance
In sunshine in the waters of the lake?
Lengthening shadows in moonlight did prance,
As by its side we lay often awake.

Those days and nights, though now in distant past
Are still fresh in my heart and in my mind.
But what a pity that you, in contrast,
Have forgotten them, what an act unkind!

Now verily I do live in the past.
Dark shadows on my future are now cast.

9th March 2007

75. A FLICKER OF LIGHT

*[As I grope and falter in darkness, He shows me light
and holds my hand]*

In darkness, hesitating, I shuttle
From one faltering step to another,
What do I see there in the dark tunnel?
A flicker of light in a far corner.

What light is that coming as a godsend
In moments of pain and gloom and despair?
I struggle towards it across a bend,
On my lips an honest and fervent prayer.

I stumble on a stone but ere I fall,
Unknowingly into a pit like hell,
The name of Lord my lips instantly call
And he holds me, from his touch I can tell.

The thought that he is always there with me,
Makes me resume with courage my journey.

9th March 2007

76. DON'T HOLD BACK
[Don't hold back your love]

Though you weigh heavy in my every thought
Yet you are not a burden on my heart.
Before meeting you I was so distraught,
I knew not where in life to make a start.

My days were spent hiding from all my shame.
I spent my nights dwelling in the time past.
A ray of hope I had not till you came.
I hope this light is now going to last.

Please don't hold back your love from me my love.
No more heartbreaks in life I can endure.
I pray that he may guide us from above,
That our love may be abiding and pure.

Let this moment our love be cemented
Lest by some evil we be prevented.

10th March 2007

77. TENDER FEELINGS

[Mutual feelings of love for each other]

I think that it's a fact that you like me.
I too have feelings of soft love for you.
Your feelings towards me are clear to see.
I too can't live without you, it is true.

Though I have never mentioned it to you,
Nor you have ever whispered it to me,
We both do seem to entertain a cue
That jointly has been planned our destiny.

My dear, I always harboured a thought that
A day will come when you will be just mine.
It's not my feeling, rather His diktat,
That our lives should together intertwine.

All that I need is just a nod from you
To colour my life in a bright new hue.

All that I need is just a nod from you
That will colour my life in a new hue.

21ˢᵗ March 2007

78. AN ODE TO LAUGHTER

*[There is much to laughter. There is scientific proof that
it peps both mind and body]*

Why laughter is called the best medicine?
Because the men of medicine do vouch
That when all the time sorrows do we spin
We are more likely to take to the couch.

Research so far does clearly mention
That patients' illness of many a type
Heals well if there is no mental tension
But worsens if depression is in hype.

All over the world we have laughter clubs.
Their popularity shows but one thing:
If you forget your sorrows and hiccups,
Both mind and the body will be in zing.

So harken, all men, laugh and be merry.
Do not all the time mental woes carry.

3rd April 2007

79. BIRTHDAY THOUGHTS

[A birthday does not bring much of a cheer to an old man]

Should I be happy it is my birthday,
As I complete today sixty five years?
I cannot with any certainty say,
I harbour only hope and have no fears.

Often the only hope old men have is,
A dependent's life he may never live.
The one thing that frightens the old is this:
When he needs, no one may attention give.

In fact, long life may not be such a boon
For old men who are crippled and diseased.
An old man wishes death may kiss him soon
And from throes of pain he may be released.

For old men death is too often welcome
When they have lived a life that is fulsome.

6th May 2007

80. THE SONNET OF THE OLD
[The old are slow but sharp]

Don't think that I am just a spent out force
Having nothing worthwhile left within me.
My life might have taken an ageing course.
Age can't cut a giant to a pigmy.

My hands may shake and my legs may totter.
I may be toothless, my grasp may be weak.
You may think that aimlessly I loiter
Silently as I have nothing to speak.

Rest assured, I observe all that's around
With eyes and mind sharp like that of an owl.
In my wisdom, I don't want to confound
Others by pointing out that things are foul.

My friend, the old may be old in body.
But stout remains their mental rhapsody.

7th May 2007

81. A BEAUTIFUL FACE
[Beauty is skin deep]

I know my friend that you are beautiful.
I know it, too, you know it more than me.
But why should you, of arrogance, be full?
My being plain is no ignominy.

Your skin is glowing and hair is silky;
Your eyes sparkle, your smile does captivate.
Why that a cause of pride for you should be
And make you, from faithfulness, vacillate?

A thing of beauty a joy forever?
That may be true of a thing, not a face.
A face is just a reflection clever.
The truth inside the heart it can't erase.

The real beauty lies inside the heart.
It's that which plays in love the real part.

17th May 2007

82. GIVE ME STRENGTH AND PEACE
[Praying to the Lord for strength and peace]

I hope a day comes when I need not live
In waters full of alligators, sharks.
To have such a day what I shall not give?
Life has so far been full of thorns and barbs.

The worldly ways are mean and devious
For which unsuited is my simple heart.
My path is lost, Lord make it obvious.
Tell me from where and how to make a start.

I gladly shall do what you have ordained
But don't forsake me when I need you so.
In waters dark I have so far sustained,
But beyond this I can no longer go.

Lord, do bestow on me your strength and peace,
So that I carry out your task with ease.

19th May 2007

83. SUMMERS AND WINTERS

[Winters in the winter of life are harder than in the summer]

I'm warmed no longer by the summers lived;
I'm worried about winters to be faced.
I soar no more now that my wings are clipped.
I hope my final walk is not ill paced.

The summer of life was really hot
But this winter is truly full of chill.
While thoughts of depression I harbour not,
To face the icy winter I lack will.

Lord, warm me when it freezes all around
So my weakened knees don't fail on the way.
Let, in my final days, your grace abound;
Guide me towards your feet and there me lay.

You made me glide in life through the summer.
Please hold my hand as I trudge through winter.

25th May 2007

84. LIVE EACH DAY

[Begin each day afresh, with new hope and faith]

Live each day happily as it unfolds.
Why carry yesterday's burden with you?
You don't know what tomorrow for you holds.
Why should about the past you always rue?

Live each season as it presents each year,
No winter is for all time here to stay.
Why should a bad today give you much fear?
Why should at all your tomorrow it sway?

"Lord, give me this day my bread", Jesus prayed,
But for the next day nothing did he ask.
On the present emphasis he had laid.
The one in hand is the important task.

So my friend, live each season as it comes.
Enjoy the tune of life that each day hums.

4th June 2007

85. EMPTY MASK

[All of us wear a mask all the time. Why not discard it?]

A mask is what we wear all the day long,
Our real feelings we hide deep within.
We pose we are saintly and do no wrong,
Though in the mind we may harbour black sin.

"Can I help you", said with a painted smile,
Often hides 'could not care less' attitude.
While thoughts we entertain inside are vile,
Outwardly we show too much gratitude.

It's true that the world is too much with us;
For this world we put on a constant show.
How we look, about this we make a fuss;
Inside we are heartless, all of us know.

It's time we reflect on it and we ask:
Should not we throw away this empty mask?

23rd June 2007

86. FANCY DRESS PARTY
[The gulf between the haves and the have- nots.]

The fancy dress show goes on in full swing,
The quetzal hat, the peacock dress, the pearls.
All wish that they a real surprise spring.
A colourful display, in fact, unfurls.

The dance and light and music captivate,
Champagne and Chivas Regal flowing free.
When bodies mingle, they don't hesitate,
In every nook and corner there's much spree.

I wish you very happy day indeed
On having sweet sixteen age now attained.
But verily my heart today does bleed.
What have you, by such royal spending, gained?

In hunger half the children their life spend.
How can this party I enjoy my friend?

23rd June 2007

87. A BEE IN HIS BONNET

[About oneself, looking back.]

About a man it is who, like Newton,
Was busy picking many a pebble,
Of knowledge at sea shore, weather-beaten.
In three different fields he did dabble.

He taught as a medical professor,
For three decades and found it rather cool.
For law he had love not a bit lesser.
After retirement he joined the law school.

He joined the bar as a lawyer and then,
He tried to hone his skills in writing verse.
He did make abundant use of his pen,
The poems he wrote had a message terse.

Looks like he had a bee in his bonnet.
He himself did write this his own sonnet.

14th July 2007

88. WHEN FRIENDS TURN INTO FOES

[When friends turn foes and all is dark...]

When friends turn into foes and all is dark,
When evil is all that raises its head;
When night is black without a glow or spark,
When one feels, more than alive, one is dead;

When silence screams louder than any voice,
When loneliness alone gives company;
When nothing but solitude is the choice,
When life is but a tragic symphony;

It's then that one knows one cannot afford
To look away from the path He has shown.
And, when one does surrender to the Lord,
By His kind touch all of the woes are gone.

Let's remember: To him who in Him lives,
He always His kind hope and His grace gives.

12th August 2007

89. MAKING WAY FOR THE YOUNG

[It is true that the old have to make way for the young.]

When not a day does pass without a groan,
And not a night does pass when I have sleep;
When my own helplessness I do bemoan,
And secretly for myself I do weep;

When no one seems to care that I exist,
It matters not whether I live or die.
Life no longer appears to be a gift.
Why be afraid of death if it is nigh?

The old should try to make way for the young.
In their time truly they enjoyed their youth.
Why should the old by their neglect be stung?
It's time the old do learn this simple truth:

The world belongs to those who're young, not old.
Let this in minds of old men yet unfold.

3rd December 2007

90. WHEN IT MATTERED
[A time comes when things cease to matter.]

Welcome my friend, my sweetheart, my lover,
Welcome to my home that is not a home.
It's true that o'er my head I have cover
But in wilderness verily I roam.

I wish you had come when my heart was young,
When inside it had a burning desire.
There was a time when love songs I had sung,
That lilted like the flames of my love fire.

But now I know my spark was one sided.
Your own embers were meant for another.
To part from me one day you decided.
From that day my life just did not matter.

You have come to a bleeding, ruined heart
Alas, it is too late to make a start.

3rd December 2007

91. HE MADE MAN IN HIS IMAGE
[If that be so, why despise men?]

We drift mindless along the flow of life,
Unsure of what we like or what we need.
We often lament world is full of strife.
But why? To this we don't pay any heed.

We spend time in petty squabbles, pursuits.
But life is precious, not to be wasted.
Whether bitter or sweet may be life's fruits,
It's important that both should be tasted.

Never are two men or women alike.
We should not hate those who are not like us.
Though different, why should we them dislike?
After all we travel in the same bus.

God made man truly in his own image.
Hence all are godly as per this adage.

24th December 2007

92. THANKS FOR NEW YEAR GREETINGS

[My response to New Year wishes]

Thanks for sending me your New Year greetings,
Though after seeing sixty-six New Years,
Happy New Year wishes are sweet nothings.
About future I don't have any fears.

Those days are gone when I did look forward,
To get greeting cards or some lovely gifts.
Now each day does slowly take me toward,
The gate from which finally man exits.

The recent years have truly made me sad,
As countries have been bombed on false pretext.
That WMD secretly they had,
Though the USA knew it's not a fact.

Let's hope New Year brings new peace in the world.
Let's hope nations and men follow God's word.

25th December 2007

93. EMPTY CUP

[When life's cup is empty, it can't be filled]

When face is wrinkled and the eyes are dim,
When people seem to talk in low whispers.
When joy seems to have drained and life is grim,
When years ahead seem too full of winters.

When joints are creaky, moving is a pain,
When days are drowsy, nights devoid of sleep.
When thoughts of future seem to be in vain,
And those of the days past do make one weep.

It's then that we realise we are old,
And no longer welcome among the young.
The world inside and outside is too cold,
And life's song seems to have been fully sung.

What should one do when one's inning is up,
When wine is not there, empty is the cup?

30th December 2007

94. DON'T BLAME FATE

[What is within our power is to do good. Fate will take care of itself]

Do good to all but never do expect,
That all will ever do good unto you.
Others' feelings you should always respect,
But don't expect it from the others too.

Selfishness is inherent in all men,
We must learn to transcend this evil trait.
Bestowed we all are with paper and pen,
Good or bad it is for us to create.

Canvas in front of us, in hand the brush,
We can paint life as we deem it is best.
We can build it and we can also crush,
It's for us to pass or fail in the test.

So harken all, never do blame the fate.
Your fate is what you yourself do create.

10th January 2008

95. WAITING UPON ONE WHO IS LEAVING

[Written for a friend waiting upon his wife]

To one who is waiting upon his wife,
As she awaits her that final moment,
When she would be free from the woe and strife,
Of this life and quit her worldly raiment.

What word of solace can a friend offer?
What sane advice a mere mortal can give?
He only his hand can gently proffer,
And hope in His grace she may ever live.

At such a time it is so hard to think,
Of something to say to the one grieving.
But silent thoughts for the one 'bout to sink,
Reach without fail the soul that is leaving.

Do not think that such prayers are no use.
Even though silent, they are quite diffuse.

24th January 2008

96. THE DOG, THE FROG AND THE THIEF

[A funny sonnet for children]

I came home once and found the door open,
And, afraid that a thief might be inside,
I walked softly and found a glass broken,
That cut my feet. To stop bleeding I tried.

But smell of fresh blood woke the sleeping dog,
Who had been lulled to sleep by the vile thief.
The glass had inside it a tiny frog,
Which now was enjoying its freedom brief.

I found the frog and put it in a jar.
Then I told the dog to find the burglar.
By this time he had not gone much too far.
I caught him tight around his big collar.

Then I put the frog down his sweaty shirt,
Along with plenty of the roadside dirt.

28th February 2008

97. DARKEST NIGHT
[Thoughts about the night of death]

When brightness of the day is almost gone,
The evening shadows loom in horizon,
The sky is full of clouds where sun had shone,
And hope has given way to derision.

When pleasures of the life are there no more,
When gloom and darkness everywhere abound,
When spirit cannot any more endure,
When not a ray of happiness is found.

Will that count as the darkest night of all?
Will that be the one full of black travail?
Will it be just a precipitous fall?
Will it be a moment without avail?

No, that won't be for me the darkest night,
As He will beckon me with kindly light.

8th March 2008

98. LAKESIDE DREAMS
[Memories of shattered dreams]

This very place is the one where I walked,
With you, hand in hand, tender thoughts in heart.
On this very bench by the lake we stopped,
And you had kissed me and our love did start.

Can I forget that turbulent moment,
Which now truly is a part of my life?
My heart had then willingly itself lent,
To dreams of being one day your sweet wife.

Those dreams were never destined to be true.
Never that love was meant to touch your heart.
Truly I was destined to that day rue,
Now knowing that you played a scheming part.

Those dreams are gone and my life is shattered.
Happy you are as if nothing mattered.

9th March 2008

99. IF I TREMBLE

[Lord, if I tremble, pick me up]

Lord help me follow the path you have shown,
So one day I reach my destination.
You know that to temptation I am prone;
Please don't visit me with consternation.

Please give me strength so that I don't falter,
Hold my hand so I don't fall into sin.
Guide me unto your heavenly altar,
Encourage me, my journey I begin.

If I tremble, let me tremble bravely,
Knowing in my heart that you're not away.
If my knees give in the path heavenly,
Pick me up but don't let me go astray.

Now that in my heart your light you have shown,
I know you are with me, I'm not alone.

19th March 2008

100. DON'T BE ATTACHED

[We will quit this world one day. Why be attached to it?]

Should I worry that one day I will go,
Never to come back to my kith and kin?
Should I future anxiety today show,
About dead silence, that will then begin.

Shall I be separated from my spouse,
Of twenty five years whom I love so well?
And also from my son, my job, my house,
In which I quite comfortably do dwell?

My part they are, so much I love them all.
But one day I will lose them without fail.
I must accept the writing on the wall.
Over the destiny I can't prevail.

It's better to be wise, not be attached,
To what one day will be surely detached.

31st March 2008

101. A WOMAN SCORNED
[Hell knows no fury like a woman scorned]

A woman scorned is a hungry tigress,
On prowl to kill the object of her hate.
Energy of a fiend she can possess,
Let none in her path hide or lie in wait.

But unlike a tigress she won't show claws,
She would instead keep smiling and look calm.
Her heart only knows it has fatal flaws,
And that her poison is disguised as balm.

God save those unwise who choose to cross her.
She knows no bounds and harbours no scruples.
Till hell she would pursue them and badger
Those who happen to hit at her knuckles.

Men be forewarned, don't harass a woman.
She can well be a pernicious omen.

NOTE: While many attribute the quote "hell hath no fury like a woman scorned" to William Shakespeare the quote is actually from the play, "The Mourning Bride" by William Congreve (1670-1729).
The complete quote is:
"Heaven has no rage like love to hatred turned,
Nor hell a fury like a woman scorned."

3rd April 2008

102. A PATH TO YOU
*[I must give up my path. Help me along the new one,
Yours]*

A path to you is what I strive to find,
So that I reach You ere my time is up.
I know that fathers are to children kind.
Please show Your kindness, fill my empty cup.

I lived like a man who thinks he's clever.
I never bothered to fulfil Your wish.
Yet I was sure it would happen never,
That without water You would keep Your fish.

But now my days remain only a few,
I wish to disengage from this world now.
I want to change my direction anew,
So that I reach You and Your grace somehow.

I seek Your pardon, Lord forgive my sins.
Please make sure that the Satan never wins.

18th April 2008

103. LIFE IS NOT DARK

[Don't despair, have a heart. After tonight, new day will start]

My friend with each breath why should you bemoan?
You need not think that life itself is dark.
Do not forget, though embers may be gone,
There lurks in ashes just a tiny spark.

You need but just a spark to have a flame,
As long as you have a burning desire.
That spark, my friend, ignites your total frame,
And truly enkindles in you a fire.

In fact, in this world short is our sojourn,
We can't afford to waste any moment.
To win this race should be our sole concern,
Though we may face too much impediment.

Arise and lift your spirits, shed your gloom.
Beyond the horizon sunlight does loom.

7th June 2008

104. THE PATH OF PEACE

*[Anger is like an acid that corrodes the vessel in which it
is kept]*

Why don't you quit this fighting attitude?
Like enemies we don't have to behave.
Why not display a serene platitude?
Why must in anger you convulse and rave?

What did you gain by being bellicose,
Except some ulcers and many a scald?
Let life be lived like poetry, not prose,
Each poem does its own beauty herald.

For only a short time this life's granted.
Make friends or enemies as per your will.
But rest assured whatever you planted,
Won't lie buried, will grow, and confront still.

My friend, it's best to tread the path of peace,
For your own happiness and mental ease.

25th June 2008

105. IMPOSTER
[Treachery in love]

You came and looked at me as if in trance,
And told me that I had bewitched you so.
You said you were maddened by my fragrance,
You told me in your heart my love did grow.

A girl I was not even yet sixteen,
While you had seen more than half of the world.
You said one like me you had never seen.
And I easily did believe your word.

This seemed to make you rather too much bold.
I thought it was just a bit of sherry.
The real truth was but yet to unfold.
You took my all by evil treachery.

I came to know too late your character.
You turned out to be just an imposter.

22nd August 2008

106. GOODBYE
[The sonnet of final goodbye]

When life is hell and living a sentence,
When death seems rather such a pleasant thing,
Then why, of living, continue pretence?
Why not have from the precipice a fling?

Why be afraid of loss of consciousness,
The prelude to a most serene silence?
The jump will last a second, even less,
And will end life's irregular cadence.

Nothing is so precious about my life.
No one will ever miss me, I am sure.
There's none to mourn me, son, daughter or wife.
For me this life was ignominy pure.

So friends, adieu, I wish you now goodbye.
My home will now be far up in the sky.

31ˢᵗ August 2008

107. A STUDENT PICKS A GUN

[About the increasing incidences of campus shootings in the USA]

When life is a purposeless existence
When mirror of the future shows nothing,
When everybody just keeps up pretence,
No ray of hope does the new sunrise bring.

Then what do the students feel in their heart?
They get disenchanted, don't want to live.
A vile chain of thoughts in their mind does start:
"Bullets to the society we shall give".

So one morning a student picks a gun,
And starts shooting whoever is around.
The job done, from the scene he does not run.
He shoots himself, a way of exit found.

When life is too materialistic,
Then morals to the conscience do not stick.

5th September 2008

108. ONLY MYSELF TO BLAME

*[I squandered what I had and spurned the poor. Now
that I am spurned, why blame others?]*

I now don't have a roof over my head.
I don't know if my next meal I will get.
I've forgotten the softness of a bed.
 My clothes are dirty, stinking, rather wet.

I too have known better days in my life.
A time was there when life to me was kind.
I knew not then of poverty and strife.
To others' woes and hardships I was blind.

The world to me is not benevolent.
For this only I myself am to blame.
Why should I feel now so much repentant?
Ups and downs are found there in every game.

My friend, save always for the rainy day.
Always to the Lord for his kindness pray.

9th September 2008

109. CHILDREN PLAYING

[Watching children at play.]

Oh, what a great pleasure it is to see,
Young children absorbed in their little games.
In their plans and thoughts they are too busy,
They mix freely, future gentlemen, dames.

Too much lost are they in their little world,
Of parents, friends, fairies, pictures and toys.
So sweet and innocent is their each word,
As they play together, the girls and boys.

It's quite a pity that they do grow old,
And get conscious of the evils around.
In dreams, no longer fairies they behold.
From skies of hope, they come down to the ground.

Though that transition is necessary,
Let it be slow without too much hurry.

11th October 2008

110. TRYING TO WAKE UP THE AWAKE
[The ignorant can be taught, not the men of learning]

Who can awake a person not asleep?
Who can make a seed grow that is barren?
It's beyond even them, they would but weep,
The kind and graceful angels of heaven.

Some people are awake but keep eyes shut.
Such childish pranks simply amuse the wise.
But learning itself seems to be bankrupt,
When men of learning prefer to close eyes.

It's axiomatic, fools may be taught,
But not those who teach loudly to others.
One who carries a lamp thinks he need not,
If none about the lamp or light bothers.

It's no use waking one who is awake.
Why give knowledge to one who thinks it's fake?

12th March 2009

111. BARTERING WISDOM

[Some march ahead where angels fear to tread...]

Some march ahead where angels fear to tread.
Some tilt at windmills Don Quixotic style.
Some in sincerity rumours do spread.
Some needlessly, to others, are hostile.

Some jot a few words randomly and claim,
That they write just wonderful poetry,
Though while writing each verse they rather maim
It of rhyme, rhythm and flow, so necessary.

The heights can't be measured by those who're low,
As depths can't be measured by those at shore.
God's grace alone can such wisdom bestow,
Which makes us think others too maybe pure.

Lord, grant me this, I pray at your altar:
For knowledge, I may not wisdom barter.

15th March 2009

112. SHADOWS: a sonnet-- award winner.

[Shadows of gloom, haunted by memories.]

When shadows darken on the horizon
And creep slowly into my broken heart,
I know too well, in my mental prison,
A night of torture is going to start.

A lonely night, remembering my life,
My days when I too was a happy man,
When I caressed fondly my loving wife,
And braved the war as leader of my clan.

The memory of those colourful days,
When I did shape my life with my own hand,
Now, hauntingly, on my lonely mind plays,
Reminding me, life is written in sand.

Forsaken by all, crippled in the mind,
No one is there to speak a word that's kind.

29th March 2009

113. WHEN WOMEN MASQUERADE

[Women masquerading as men degrade womanhood]

When women masquerade as men they think,
That they have gained a hand against the men.
But what they need probably is a shrink.
Womanhood's loss is not a good omen.

Equalling men in calling dirty names,
Challenging them openly in duel,
Rubbing shoulders with them in raucous games,
Are all, on feminism, a joke cruel.

Let not women overlook this truth then,
That men are brusque, women gentle and sweet.
If they want to earn the respect of men,
From vile masculine traits they must retreat.

What wins a man's heart is delicacy.
Shed confrontation, use diplomacy.

2nd April 2009

114. BETTER YIELD TO FOOLS

[When ignorance is bliss, it is folly to be wise]

No I shall not allow myself to be,
By fools lured into unseemly duel.
Of my words and thoughts they are not worthy,
For whom intelligence is too cruel.

The wise have said clearly since days of yore:
Avoid the fools, do not argue with them.
You will otherwise lose mental peace your,
When fools create nonsensical mayhem.

When ignorance is bliss, why be then wise?
When wisdom is a curse, why display it?
By arguing with fools we pay a price:
The men of credit come to discredit.

Better keep them at a full arm's distance.
But don't anger them, keep up a pretence.

4ᵗʰ April 2009

115. MANLY V. WOMANLY

[A satire upon those prone to say: "Come on, fight like a man."]

Is it manly to pick a gun and shoot,
Or womanly to rather prefer calm?
Whatever be, but it is rather brute,
To wield the machete rather than the balm.

Instead of talking, why itch for a fight?
For wise people that's not how to behave.
Of logical discussion, why make light?
Why hedge around the point and rant and rave?

Those who move about challenging people,
Are not too manly, ask your own conscience.
Why be happy snooping like a beagle,
Looking for signs of a tiny offence?

If fighting others be a manly trait,
A world without fighting men would be great.

9th April 2009

116. CALLING NAMES

*[Those who simply call names or abuse others, debase
themselves]*

Some people call others many a name,
And think this raises them in others' eyes.
In doing so they feel not any shame.
Merrily they indulge in their wild cries.

The caravan moves on irrespective,
Of dogs that keep on barking so freely.
But they who're sure of their own perspective,
Carry on in their quest relentlessly.

O God, show this kindness to your children,
That they may see you in your countless shapes.
Let them not call names but be beholden,
To those whom your majesty itself makes.

Lord when I go, let this be said of me:
He was a friend to all, none's enemy.

5th May 2009

117. KNOW, BUT DON'T TELL SO
[Know more than others if you can, but don't tell them so]

I came across a wonderful advice:
"Work hard and learn all that there is to know.
But never develop this useless vice,
Of telling others you are learned so."

Men and women want to think they know much.
Why deny them their innocent pleasure?
If dreams of riches make them happy such,
Let poor people conjure wealth at leisure.

Real wisdom lies in following this:
"Know more than others if you ever can.
Earn riches to fulfil your every wish,
But look at riches rather with disdain."

A mind that is ever tranquil, at peace,
Will be in final moments quite at ease.

5th May 2009

118. TIME MARCHES ON

[Time never stops. Don't regret the lost moments. Move with time]

Time marches on, no two moments are same.
What now is will be no more next moment.
We all know this but still it is a shame,
We cling to old memories and lament.

Why try to recreate old times somehow?
Why cling to the events already past?
Why love too much the moment that is now,
Why stop it knowing full well it can't last?

I don't say we should not value the old.
All I say is don't grieve over the loss.
What matters is inner substance, the gold,
Not outwardly shine or fragrance or gloss.

None can prevent the onward march of time.
It's better to make our own lives sublime.

22nd July 2009

119. AMENDS

[A pasted sorry or a smile, if not sincere, can be quite vile]

No cancer can be cured by just a pill.
A moment of love cannot wash neglect.
A single step can't take us up the hill.
Good wish cannot save a murder suspect.

A life full of sin can't be wished away.
A smile cannot lessen the pain of knife.
Without a candle there can't be a ray.
Amends cannot absolve unfaithful wife.

My friend, better be watchful and don't fall,
Into the dark bottomless pits of hell.
Your entreaties there will fail one and all.
The way to come out of it none can tell.

Why not follow the straight and simple way?
Let not the wayside charms lead you astray.

16th August 2009

120. DESIRE AND HOPE
[Why harbour desires for which there is no hope?]

No less painful are barbs if they're disguised,
Thorns carrying rose fragrance are yet sharp.
Poison kills, even though with wine imbibed,
Foes remain foes though of friendship they harp.

Ungratefulness is not undone by smiles.
The killers do not have a change of heart.
A journey planned for a few thousand miles,
Remains a dream if we don't make a start.

Appearance is often quite deceptive.
Good intentions are often circumspect.
To every sweet word, don't be receptive,
In world today even friends are suspect.

We may make every possible effort,
But we can't make it rain in a desert.

16th August 2009

121. BLUNT ARROWS
[Arrows that boomerang hurt only the archer]

Why not ignore the one you do not like?
Why call him names, insult him for nothing?
What use it is if someone you do strike,
But arrows just return back to your sling?

The barbs and thorns hurt only the one who,
Grabs them and takes them direct to his heart,
But if that person simply ignores you,
It shows that he is much wiser and smart.

Why get frustrated in a manner thus,
That your arrows just do not penetrate?
If you ride mistakenly the wrong bus,
Your destination will not be your fate.

Why harm and humiliate another,
In fact, about this, who does not bother?

25th August 2009

122. WHAT FIRE CAN WARM A HEART

[One must not be daunted by adversity. Both joys and sorrows are a part of life]

What fire can warm a heart that is frozen?
What spark can enliven one that's silent?
What wave can move a heart that has chosen,
To remain still, never to be vibrant?

What light can brighten a heart that is dark?
What softness can melt feelings that are hard?
What joy can vanquish a gloom that is stark?
What fate can bring prize to a luckless card?

A positive frame of mind is required,
To get over grief and a sullen mood.
Let not mind be in worries always mired.
Man cannot gain if always he does brood.

No man's life is always joyful, perfect.
That we are all imperfect is a fact.

20th February 2009

123. WOMEN AND SEA

[Both share similar traits]

Why compare a woman to the sea?
Because they share comparable traits,
Woman, tempestuous can sure she be,
When she is angry on one whom she hates.

Women's eyes can be unfathomable.
They have a gaze that is too sharp and deep.
They can, like sea, be uncontrollable.
They shed salty tears when they cry and weep.

Of this fact all men are too well informed:
Both can be calm and furious at times.
"Hell has no fury like a woman scorned",
Thus wrote Congreve about feminine crimes.

Though men may claim they have mastered the sea,
Few would venture to say this of a she.

28th January 2010

124. A LOST LOVE
[A love cut short by the sea]

This sea on whose shore I do walk today,
Pensively trotting, watching gentle waves,
Was not so calm that day it took away,
My wife and I learnt how it ill behaves.

I was then a newly married husband,
She was proud of her aquatic prowess.
She went out swimming far away from sand,
So that her husband she may well impress.

She went too far and was overpowered,
By waves that rose up like a tsunami.
My calls to her were not probably heard.
She disappeared, never returned to me.

I pine to meet her but there is no way.
For my lost love, I walk the shore today.

24th February 2010

125. BALLOONS AND MOMENTS

[They are both fleeting. Let them fly. Don't hold on to them.]

The days and events are like gas balloons,
That go up once never to return back,
Their memories may return like typhoons,
And bring back those moments that now we lack.

When we release the balloons in the sky,
We let them go off without further thought.
Why don't the same principle we apply,
And let old memories bother us not?

It's better to let bygones be bygones,
And not ponder too much on moments past.
Remember that no one in the world moans,
For those who can't their mental burden cast.

My friend, do not hold on to old moments.
Freedom in life such a habit prevents.

26th February 2010

126. FRUITS OF ADVERSITY
[A life of want is better than one without it]

Where one has got everything one may need,
And one need not labour to earn one's bread,
Where one, to work, need not ever pay heed,
Where comforts are, for all, so freely spread;

That place may be the one someone may like,
To live quite happily throughout his life.
But then in the mind such a thought does strike,
What worth is life without its stress and strife?'

It's stress and want that make us work and get,
Something that lessens our difficulties.
It's only when we miss something and fret,
That we put to use all our faculties.

The fruits of adversity are, yes, sweet.
Worthless is life that's with comforts replete.

18th March 2010

127. INSPIRATION

[A poet never lacks inspiration. The feelings are the inspiration]

Do I need inspiration for writing,
A haiku or a ghazal or sonnet?
No, not when themes galore are inviting,
And make me blow my poetic trumpet.

A poem is a feeling of the heart,
And my heart is never without feeling.
Expressing feelings in words is an art.
In fact, such art gives a touch of healing.

All I need is a pencil or a pen,
And paper and a few minutes of time.
Sure enough, the thoughts of the heart ripen,
And flow out in a perfect rhythm and rhyme.

It may not match a Milton or Wordsworth,
But for me the effort itself is worth.

18th March 2010

128. ON LEAVING SIXTY NINE BEHIND
[On completing 69 years]

As I enter the seventieth year,
Of my sojourn on this planet called earth,
I march ahead without a trace of fear,
Though old, I am full of vigour and mirth.

It's not that god of wealth on me does smile,
Or that I am robust like a young man.
It's only that in the Obama style,
I do believe I am young and I can.

I built an edifice of sixty nine,
Storeys that will ultimately tumble.
Yet Lord, I will sing songs of glory thine,
I care not if my body does crumble.

You gave me all that I was worthy of.
I don't need any more to, well, show off.

23rd January, 2011

NOTE: Written on 23rd January, 2011, my 70th birthday.

129. WHEN I AM GONE

[How others would remember me when I am gone]

When I shed mortal frame and I am gone,
Let this they say for sake of whom I lived:
"He always looked as if too woebegone,
Almost on purpose joy he always missed."

He never talked and kept a low profile,
Except on occasions driven by whim,
But silently he did work all the while.
He helped all those who ever came to him.

A jolly fellow he was, though morose.
Often he was the proverbial meek.
Petals and thorns he carried like a rose.
Of selflessness he had a pretty streak.

We wish so, his friends and his family,
In netherworld he may live happily."

4th September 2012

130. BROKEN SAILS
[We realise our mistakes when it is too late]

At one time I used to admire you so,
When I met you once in the path of life.
In this soft path I allowed weeds to grow,
Rendering it full of much stress and strife.

I lost my calm and equanimity.
I blamed you alone for all the travails.
I forgot that it is winds' enmity

That rips apart the strongest of ship sails.

One day the ship floundered in raging storms.
I found that I had lost all that I had.
The fault was mine, I'd broken all the norms.
This fact made me truly all the more sad.

It's better that we regret in youth prime,
Than too late in the ordained march of time.

6th September 2012

131. WHY AM I HAPPY?

*[It is God's kindness to keep an old man capable of
working hard. Work gives pleasure]*

A friend one day put me in a tight fix,
He asked how I remained happy in life,
Because in the year nineteen ninety six
I lost, of twenty five years, my sweet wife.

He wondered why I work when I'm retired,
(You see, he is exactly half my age).
He knows not old men's hearts, too, can be fired.
I hope he works when he reaches my stage.

To work does not mean having stress or pain,
It shows God's kindness that I can still work.
An idle life I would hold in disdain.
Why from doing work should I ever shirk?

I thank God He chose me to make His tool,
And trained my heart in His heavenly school.

NOTE: Written in response to what a young Indian
engineer, 35, in USA wrote to me while chatting- "You
live pretty much independently, you work hard even
while being retired, you toil day and night without a
companion and yet you smile through it all. What
resilience, Sir."

7th September 2012

132. WE MET JUST A FEW TIMES
[The fickleness of life]

We met just a few times but those times are,
The only memories I have of you.
On my heart time has left a gnawing scar,
To erase which nothing I can now do.

Those days were pristine, hearts beating with love,
Singing a tune that seemed so eternal.
None knew that far away in skies above,
It was settled you are too ephemeral.

While I set out to meet you at the lake,
Midway I was along the lovely drive,
But fate for you had too scary a take,
Your boat toppled and you could not survive.

That scene, those memories, those pangs of heart,
Will not let me a new life ever start.

20th September 2012

133. WE WON'T KNOW BEAUTY WITHOUT UGLINESS

[We appreciate the value of something only when we are deprived of it]

We won't know beauty without ugliness,
Without thirst there won't be quenching feeling.
We would not know pleasure without duress,
Without illness we won't know what's healing.

The worth of success we know through failure,
The thrill of winning knows he who has lost.
A broken heart yearns for love that is pure.
The spring is welcome after snow and frost.

Don't argue why God has created pain,
Or which is better, flower or a thorn.
Don't look down on the lowly with disdain.
Did not the crown of thorns Jesus adorn?

The God is bountiful, he has no dearth,
But gives us only that what we are worth.

08th July 2022